Original title:
Cacti Conversations

Copyright © 2025 Creative Arts Management OÜ
All rights reserved.

Author: Penelope Hawthorne
ISBN HARDBACK: 978-1-80581-727-7
ISBN PAPERBACK: 978-1-80581-254-8
ISBN EBOOK: 978-1-80581-727-7

The Unyielding Exchange

In a desert chat, prickly pals meet,
With humor so sharp, it's hard to beat.
They poke fun at the sun's blazing glare,
While sipping on water, without a care.

One says, "I'm growing old and round!"
The other replies, "You're just well-bound!"
They laugh and jibe, in their spiky attire,
In their pointy world, they both conspire.

Conversations Under the Sun

Under the sun, two plants exchange,
Funny tales of life, both wild and strange.
One claims to dance under the moonlight,
While the other just buzzes, a pure delight.

They swap jokes of a lizard so sly,
Who thinks he can dance, but just can't fly.
With laughter surrounding each leaf and spine,
These bold little greens know just how to shine.

Whispers in the Wilderness

In the wild, where the sunflowers sway,
Two prickle-friends decide to play.
"Did you hear of the cactus who went for a swim?"
"Oh please, that idea was truly grim!"

They chuckle at tales of a needle's plight,
In a world filled with laughs, they shine so bright.
Whispers are shared beneath the blue sky,
And the desert blooms, as time wanders by.

From Thorns to Thoughts

From sharp thorns to thoughts that spark,
Two clever cacti laugh in the dark.
"What's softer than a cloud in the day?"
"Your jokes, my friend, seem to keep foes at bay!"

With every quip, they blossom anew,
Finding humor in each drop of dew.
To the rhythm of rustling in the breeze,
These spiky wisecrackers are sure to tease.

The Unspoken Bond

In a garden where prickly pals reside,
Silent giggles in the sun, they hide.
A nod of a spines, a sway with glee,
Who knew plants could frolic so freely?

Whispered jokes about the heat, they share,
Holding secrets that dance in the air.
A prick here, a poke just for fun,
These sharp-tongued friends having a pun!

Dialogues at Dusk

At twilight's edge, they start their chat,
A dialogue soft, with a witty pat.
Under the glow of a fading light,
They swap tall tales, oh what a sight!

"Look at me, I stand so tall!"
"And I'm round and proud, can't you see?" they call.
With humorous banter and playful jive,
These tough little ones sure come alive!

In the Shade of Resilience

Beneath the leaves, they gather in shade,
Spiky comrades where fun's never delayed.
With roots intertwined, a jest or two,
Weathering storms, their laughter's the glue.

"Come, let's poke fun at the rain," they sigh,
"Despite the drops, we're still spry!"
In this refuge, not a care to be found,
For joy blooms bravely on solid ground.

Nature's Quiet Exchange

Amongst the thorns, a party unseen,
In a prickly elegy, they laugh like a dream.
With humor stitched in their woven roots,
They trade shy winks in their playful suits.

In whispers low, the night does unfold,
Stories of sunshine, both warm and bold.
For under the stars, they happily conspire,
To tickle the fancies of those who inquire.

Resilience: A Living Poem

In a desert so dry, with a spiky face,
These green fellows stand, holding their place.
With a wink and a nod, they say, "Aren't we grand?"
While sipping the sun, they enjoy their own brand.

With arms wide open, they dance in the heat,
Swaying to tunes, with no shoes on their feet.
"Who needs a rain dance?" they chuckle with glee,
"Just give us some sunshine, and we're happy as can be!"

When the winds come a-howlin' and the storms start to brew,
They stand firm and sturdy, like a bouncer in blue.
"Bring on your tempests, we're ready to play!"
While laughing at clouds that dare block their ray.

So here's to the green, with their armor so tough,
They teach us a lesson: life can get rough.
But with a bit of humor, and some sunlight to share,
We can all stand our ground, without worry or care.

Nature's Resilient Voice

In desert attire, they joke with the sun,
With needles and quirks, it's all in good fun.
Sharing tall tales of drought and of rain,
While wagging their arms at the clouds in disdain.

They drink up the laughs in the heat of the day,
With roots that are anchored, they always will stay.
Sipping on sunshine, they shout with glee,
"Who needs a fountain? Just look at me!"

Echoing in the Expanse

A tall one stood up, saying, "Watch my flair!"
The round one replied, "I can spin in mid-air!"
They chuckled and wiggled, poking fun at their looks,
As the lizards nearby turned to read all the books.

When shadows grew long, they planned a dance,
To sway in the breeze, oh, what a romance!
With prickly performance on stage of blue sky,
They pulled off their stunts, oh my, oh my!

Distant Murmurs

In distant gardens, whispers take flight,
"You call that a hug? You're prickly, not tight!"
Giggles echo off rocks, a soft hidden sound,
As their humor spreads wide, like roots underground.

Plant pals share secrets under the moon,
"I swear, it was a cactus that danced to a tune!"
They poke fun at the cacti who stand out in rows,
While the stars wink and nod, part of this show.

Speaking in Silence

In stillness they grin, with humor untold,
Each spine has a story, each laugh worth its gold.
With puns on their petals, they raise a cheer,
A rustling reminder that laughter is near.

They watch as the sun dips, an audience grand,
"Tonight's the performance, come take a stand!"
With shadows for partners, they begin their play,
Underneath the vast sky, they steal hearts away.

Secrets Shared in Sandy Shadows

In the desert's hug, we laugh, oh so sly,
Prickly tales stir, as the lizards glide by.
A sunburned sage whispers, 'It's too dry!'
While gophers plot mischief without a sigh.

We spin our yarns under a sunbeam's glance,
Chortling about our pointy romance.
With each spiky joke, we take a stance,
In this sandy theatre, we laugh and dance.

Mutual Solitude in the Sun's Embrace

We stand apart but share the same ray,
Sticking our necks out in a peculiar way.
Poking fun at the heat that makes us sway,
While shadows laugh softly, dreaming of play.

A chuckle or two in the sunshine's glare,
Is better than nothing, or a burst of air.
We each have our needles, but none seems to care,
For a giggle's the glue in this prickly affair.

Radiant Colors of Uneasy Friendship

With hues of green mixed with worry and cheer,
We swap silly stories while sidestepping fear.
A blossom refuses to shed a tear,
For laughter is loud, when companionship's near.

The blooms itch for gossip beneath the bright sun,
While prickles debate if this friendship's begun.
Colors collide in a humorous run,
As we dance in the breeze, ever so fun.

Gestures in the Grit of the Green

In the spiny crowd, we wave with delight,
Making faces that could start a cactus fight.
A tilt of the head, it's a curious sight,
As we blend our mischief with sheer, silly might.

We shuffle through gravel, with giggles all round,
Breaking the silence, our laughter is found.
With gestures that sparkle like gems in the ground,
We forge our friendship, so awkwardly bound.

Green Thickets

In the desert sun, they stand so bright,
Waving their arms in a prickly delight.
Calling to birds with a fun little dance,
Hoping one day for a chance at romance.

But when a breeze blows, they sway and jest,
"Hey, watch your step! We're not like the rest!"
Laughter erupts from their spiky parade,
As they poke fun at the path that they made.

Prickly Encounters

Two spines met one day on a dusty road,
One said, "Hey buddy, let's lighten the load!"
"I hear your style is sharp, yet quite chic,
Let's share some tales—what do you speak?"

"Well, I once had a sunbath that went all wrong,
Came out too crispy; I was out for so long!"
The other chimed in with a giggle so grand,
"At least you had sun; I just got a tan!"

Conversations with Resilience

In arid lands where the laughter flows,
Spiky companions see how humor grows.
"We're tough,' they say, 'but we jest with cheer,
Each thorn a reminder that joy's always near!"

A wise old shrub with wisdom to spare,
Said, "Lessons come sweet from the prickles we bear.
Embrace every jab and laugh at the plight,
For humor weaves daylight through the darkest of nights!"

Thorns Speak Softly

A prickly friend mused under the sun,
"Why are we seen as less than just fun?"
With a chuckle, they tossed their green arms wide,
"Our humor's sharp, with nothing to hide!"

So they hosted a party with sun hats galore,
Joking with shadows and aching to soar.
At the end of the day, they laughed till they cried,
Finding joy in their quirkiness, side by side.

Hidden Narratives

In the desert's swelter, spines collide,
Lively tales in prickly pride.
A sagebrush laughs, it tells a joke,
While bouncing beetles spin and poke.

A stand of green with thickened skin,
Whispers secrets; grin for grin.
Chatter 'bout the moonlit night,
And how the stars can cause a fright.

The lizard pops in; has a say,
"Why don't we have a party today?"
With watermelons and sweetened tea,
The sun beats down, but we're so free!

All around, the thorns like swords,
But laughter cuts through like gentle chords.
In hidden corners, mischief plays,
While prickly pals weave silly ballets.

Dialogue of the Dust

In the heat where shadows dwell,
Dry winds carry tales to tell.
Two tumbleweeds roll and sway,
As they gossip the day away.

A saguaro grins, it's quite the sight,
Says, "Why can't we dance tonight?"
But the cholla chimes in with a sigh,
"Careful now, I've got my spikes on high!"

The ground cracks open, laughter brews,
As lizards punch in with silly views.
"Let's start a contest, the best cartwheel!
I'll give it a whirl, just to seal the deal!"

Dust whirls up, a jubilant start,
As prickly pals join in the art.
Their antics spread, no laughter missed,
In this dry expanse, joy can't be dismissed.

Conversations in Bloom

In the bright sun, blooms do chat,
"Look at me, I'm where it's at!"
A poppy bursts with vibrant cheer,
While a cactus neighbor rolls an eye, my dear.

"Whoa now, friend, it's not a race,
I'm the sturdy one with style and grace!"
Petals giggle and sway with flair,
"Let's all agree, we're all quite rare!"

A wise old herb joins in the fun,
"If we're together, we've already won!"
Their chatter blooms in colors bright,
Turning desert dunes into pure delight.

Underneath the blaring sun,
Every bloom just loves to run.
In whispered tones, they scheme and plot,
Creating magic in this lovely spot.

Tales from the Arid Expanse

In the arid land where laughter sings,
Spiky tales wear vibrant rings.
A javelina trots with a grin,
"Have you heard where the fun begins?"

The agave laughs, "I've got a plan!
Let's throw a bash for the whole clan!"
The sun may blaze, the heat may choke,
But when we gather, it's no hoax!

A jumping jackrabbits hops around,
Bringing news that's quite profound.
"The sand's a dance floor; hear the beat,
With every bounce, we'll move our feet!"

As the starlit sky begins to glow,
The spiny crew puts on a show.
With giggles, winks, and playful jests,
In this dry expanse, joy truly rests.

Unspoken Affections of the Desert Bloom

In a garden where prickles reign,
Two succulents share their pain.
One says, "You look quite sharp today,"
The other sighs, "Well, go away!"

Sunshine beams on their spiky fate,
Yet love blooms in their own mate.
With every poke and playful jab,
They laugh at each thorny drab.

Amidst the sands, they secretly dream,
Of a world where they can beam.
But their love is stuck on a shelf,
Practicing how to be themselves.

So under the sun, they might just sway,
Two furry friends in their thorny ballet.
With a wink and a twist, they embrace the fun,
Who knew such joy could sprout in the sun?

Thorny Truths Beneath the Surface

In a world that's dry and tough,
Two plants debate just who is buff.
One boasts, "I have the mightiest spikes!"
The other chuckles, "You're just like bikes!"

They'll roll and tumble without a care,
But leave a mark, oh, beware!
With humor sharp as each prickly end,
They jest like old pals who just won't bend.

"I'm deep-rooted, wise beyond years!"
One brags while the other sneers.
"Wisdom grows from soaking up sun!"
"Maybe, but I'm still the fun one!"

With laughter that echoes through the heat,
These thorns stir up quite the sweet feat.
So when they argue, it's a spectacle right,
Just two prickly pals in a desert delight!

Echoes of Resilience in the Sand

In a land where dryness reigns,
Two spiky souls share their pains.
One says, "I stand tall, wide and proud!"
The other quips, "Just blend with the crowd!"

Sandstorms blow, they laugh and sway,
"Let's not wilt, we'll find our way!"
With roots like confidence, deep and bold,
They weather the jests, forever unfold.

Each night, they plot their grand escape,
Arguing over the ideal shape.
One wants to dance, the other to chill,
But together they climb every hill.

With each tomorrow, they find their groove,
Existing life's spices, making moves.
In their stubbornness, a bond is spun,
Echoes of humor, sticking like gum!

Conversations Under the Desert Moon

Under a sky of twinkling lights,
Two spiky friends share their delights.
One cries, "The moon is just like me!"
The other laughs, "You're pricklier, you see!"

They swap their tales, both strange and vast,
Between the craters, their voices cast.
Discussing longings, they tease and jest,
With each little prick, they feel more blessed.

From sunbaked dreams to moonlit stunts,
In this desert, they find the fun bunch.
Trading secrets while basking in glow,
"Let's see who can put on the best show!"

So under the stars, they plot and scheme,
Laughing together, all in a dream.
With each follow-up, they shift and groove,
In the night's glow, their friendship moves!

Green Guardianship

In the desert, standing tall,
Prickly pals have seen it all.
Joking with the breeze in tow,
Spines keep secrets; who would know?

Sipping sunlight, sipping shade,
Trading tales of how they've stayed.
A tumbleweed rolls by with flair,
"Watch your back, there's thorns in air!"

Roots deep down in sandy lands,
Stretching out with leafy hands.
They chuckle when the raindrops fall,
"More for us! We'll have a ball!"

Beneath the stars, they share their fears,
"Will we survive another year?"
A jig of joy in moonlit nights,
Their prickly humor feels just right!

The Conversation of Shadows

In dusky light, the giants speak,
Shadows dance, a game of peek.
Casting giggles, whispers float,
Their humor wears a spiky coat.

A lizard laughs, joins in their jest,
"Who told you shades should be the best?"
"We're the kings of cool tonight!"
Swaying gently in delight.

A rabbit hops, lends an ear,
"Gentle spines, I come near dear.
Share your tales, so sharp and bright,
We'll tickle the dark, take flight!"

But shadows fade, as dawn creeps in,
"Oh well, let's do it all again!"
With laughter, they bid adieu,
The sun will find them, it's true!

Touching the Earth

In the sand, they gather round,
Spiky friends from thorny ground.
"Let's have fun, and roll about!"
They giggle, stretch, and twist about.

A tumble here, a tumble there,
"Who knew we'd be the life of air?"
With roots entwined, they share their dreams,
And plot to glow in moonlit beams.

A breeze whispers through their spines,
Creating laughter, clever lines.
"With each bump, we grow so wise!"
They tease each other, oh, what a surprise!

To touch the earth and dance with glee,
Each prickly sage shares joy, you see.
In their world of funny quirks,
Life's a trip; who knows what works?

Reflections in the Sand

As the sun sets, shadows play,
In the dunes, they have their say.
"Look at us, all lined up nice!"
Quirky lines, no need for dice.

They chat of days when clouds were light,
And stormy nights that gave a fright.
"But here we stand, forever bold,"
Their laughter sings, a tale retold.

With every grain, a new surprise,
Beneath their spines, wisdom lies.
"Let's take selfies with the stars!"
They grumble, steal, and shout, "No cars!"

The moon reflects their silly ways,
And in the dark, hilarity stays.
In sandy beds, they settle down,
These prickly jesters are the crown!

Beneath the Surface: Heartbeats in the Heat

Out in the sun, we share our tales,
With prickly laughs and breezy gales.
Dancing shadows on dry, cracked earth,
We ponder life with spiky mirth.

When desert winds bring whispers near,
We chuckle loud, dispelling fear.
In laughter's shade, we find our touch,
Who knew our hearts could bloom so much?

With little feet and spiky shoes,
We wander paths that we can't lose.
What silly sights, we jump and sway,
In sunshine bright, we play all day.

So here we sit, with arms out wide,
In this warm glow, we take our pride.
No prickly end could break our cheer,
With every joke, we buddy near.

Spiny Affections in Bloom

Among the stones, our humor sprouts,
In every poke, a laugh about.
Finding joy in every thorn,
Who knew such love could be reborn?

With a wink, we trade our pricks,
Spinning yarns with silly tricks.
In the heat, our spirits rise,
Like blooms unfolding 'neath blue skies.

Oh, the stories that we share,
With every nudge, we show we care.
A dance beneath that fiery glow,
Just watch us jive, oh how we flow!

So come and sit, let laughter bloom,
In this wild land, we find a room.
With spiny hugs and chuckles bright,
We bask together in pure delight.

Sunlit Soliloquies of the Succulent

In sunlit moments, we confide,
With winks and jests, we take a ride.
The world's so big, yet here we sit,
Trading tales in endless wit.

With every sunbeam's gentle tease,
We share our quirks; we do as we please.
Oh, how we giggle and sway,
In this bright light, we seize the day.

As curvy shadows stretch and yawn,
We revel in the coming dawn.
Life feels sweet with friends so dear,
Each silly joke brings us a cheer.

So here's to fun beneath the sun,
Where prickly hearts can always run.
In every jest, we find a tune,
Dancing together until the moon.

Parched Perspectives Under a Fiery Sky

In the blazing heat, we crack a grin,
With parched tongues, the laughter begins.
Who knew the sun could lift our woes?
We trade our quirks with clever prose.

Beneath a sky of fiery hue,
We jest and jest, inventing new.
Silly pranks and jolly shouts,
Echo through the drought and doubts.

With every twist and turning path,
We double over in hearty laughs.
In tepid air, we find our song,
What seems so wrong can't be too long!

So let's embrace this sunny fate,
With spines and smiles, it's never late.
Together, here, we spin and twirl,
In dry embrace, let's rock the world.

Thorns of Conversation and Comfort

In the desert sun, a prickly chat,
Two spiky friends wore hats so flat.
They joked about their pointy days,
And shared their tales in a sunny haze.

A tumbleweed rolled by with flair,
It bumped their knees with nary a care.
"You think it's wise to share a laugh?"
"Only if we don't make a gaffe!"

At sunset's glow, they shared their dreams,
Like sipping teas, or so it seems.
Though covered in thorns, their hearts were light,
In this silly dance of the desert night.

With giggles and jests, they set the tone,
In their own little world, they felt at home.
As stars ignited in the dusky sky,
They shared more laughter, oh my, oh my!

Exchanges in a World of Dust

In a land where sand dunes swayed,
Two quirky plants began to trade.
One had sun hats, bright and bold,
The other shared stories that never got old.

"I'll give you shade for a tale or two,"
Said the prickly pear with a grin so true.
"How about a sip from my dewdrop cup?"
"Only if you promise not to hiccup!"

As gusts of wind made the petals swirl,
They talked of rain in a parched world.
"What if it rains?" asked the little bud.
"Then we'll float like boats in the mud!"

Laughter echoed across the land,
With every jab, every funny hand.
In a world of dust, friendships bloom bright,
With exchanges that fill the starry night.

Desert Whispers

Underneath the wide, blue sky,
Two prickly pals let laughter fly.
"Did you hear about the ailing sage?"
"They say he's now a jolly mage!"

Whispers danced through the arid air,
Of humor shared without a care.
With jokes of sand and scorpion's fuss,
They turned their woes into giant plus!

They swapped their lives in funny jests,
With happy hearts and aimless quests.
"I'd trade my skin for a sweet embrace,"
"Only if you promise, not to poke my face!"

Oh, the joy in this barren stretch,
Every giggle was so well matched.
For in every whisper, in every cheer,
Stronger bonds grew, year after year.

Spines and Secrets

In a quiet patch, two spines conspired,
Each secret shared left them inspired.
"What's the burrow's best-kept lore?"
"That the dunes are just a sandy floor!"

They chuckled hard, they rolled with glee,
Trading secrets with infectious spree.
"How do you twirl when the winds are strong?"
"Like a dancer, though I can't last long!"

With every quip and every tease,
They spun their tales with effortless ease.
"Let's dream of rainbows in this heat,
And sip on dreams of a sugary treat!"

In that prickly realm, friendship bloomed,
As laughter sprang from the hearts they groomed.
Spines held wisdom, sweet and clever,
Creating memories that would last forever.

Prickly Whispers in the Desert

In the heat of the blazing sun,
Two spiky friends just having fun.
They poke and tease, they play a game,
'You're looking sharp!' one calls out with fame.

'Oh please, dear friend, I'm more than that,
I'm a cushion soft, look at my hat!'
They chuckle and shake, they wobble and sway,
As the lizards nearby join in the play.

With every jab and silly jest,
They grin and giggle, no time for rest.
In a prickly patch, they find the glee,
Life's a joke, come laugh with me!

Under stars that twinkle and glide,
They share their thoughts, with no need to hide.
In the desert, where silence can creep,
These whispers of humor never sleep!

Dialogue among Thorny Sentinels

Two sentinels stand, tall and proud,
Gossiping loudly, attracting a crowd.
One says, 'Did you hear the news today?
The sun's so hot, it might melt away!'

The other chuckles, 'That's quite the thought!
But it's just sunburn that we've all fought!'
They share their tales of the shifting sands,
Exchanging jokes and waving their hands.

A passing owl gives them a squint,
'You two are odd; is that a hint?'
But they just laugh, with spines all aglow,
In their world of humor, they'll steal the show!

As the breeze tickles their thorny tips,
Their banter flows and never slips.
In the quiet night, they're never lone,
For friendship blooms on a prickly throne!

Lessons from the Arid Heart

In the middle of a sandy patch,
Two wise ones gathering to hatch.
'What's the secret of staying so cool?'
One grins wide, 'Just play the fool!'

They trade some tales of the days gone by,
Of cactus waltzes and a sky-high fly.
'You've got to poke fun, but not too hard,
Or you may find yourself in a prickly yard!'

They share a laugh about the rains they've missed,
One sighs, 'Oh well, just add some mist!'
With a wink and a nod, they twist and shout,
'Life's too short to be filled with doubt!'

And as the sun sets on the barren land,
Their wisdom travels, hand in hand.
In the arid heart, love's lessons start,
Two funny friends, with a joyous heart!

Silent Serenades in the Sun

Beneath the sun, they gather near,
With silent smiles, they spread good cheer.
'Fancy a dance?' one whispers slow,
'This desert floor is the place to go!'

They shimmy and shake, in a quirky way,
Graceful as dunes on a windy day.
A bold adventure, with laughter their song,
Echoing softly, all day long.

'What's the scoop, dear friend of mine?'
'The sun is bright, but we will shine.'
Their conversations glow like a summer's eve,
In a world where the skies dance and weave.

And as the shadows begin to blend,
Their friendship is clear; it will not end.
Under the sun, where silence may reign,
Funny serenades ease all the pain!

Scribbles of Survival in Spines

With a poke and a nudge, we exchange our thoughts,
Our spines are a cushion, despite the pricks we brought.
Laughing at the storms that dance on our tips,
We sip on the sunshine, taking life's sips.

Silly little jokes hang in the dry air,
Who knew we could chat without a single care?
Each thorn a storyteller, each spike a delight,
In our tiny green world, we share laughable sights.

When the sun beats down and the shadows retreat,
We shift our positions, make room for our feet.
Wagging our needles like some wild, crazy crew,
"Hey there, did you hear that? A squirrel's passing through!"

So here is our tale in the desert's bold hue,
A party of one, yet two can pull through.
In this sun-soaked haven, oh, what a sight,
Our prickled remarks make the long days seem bright.

The Language of Stillness in the Heat

When the sun's overhead, we say not a word,
But oh, the warm silence is truly absurd.
Wiggling our arms, we do a little dance,
In the stillness of heat, we take our stance.

We exchange our quirks like secret hand signs,
With a tilt and a turn, fun twists in our vines.
Imitating shadows that flutter and sway,
We're a bunch of green comedians, here to play.

Even as the temperature starts to rise,
We laugh at the tricks the desert applies.
Gossip of breezes, we humorously share,
The tumbleweeds rolling—oh, what a flare!

So raise a spiked glass to the sun and the fun,
Each day in the heat seems never quite done.
In this standing-room-only, we giggle and cheer,
For the language of stillness reveals what is dear.

Unraveled Stories of Drought

In the dry of the land, there's a humor that flows,
With each wilting leaf, the laughter still grows.
We swap tales of rain with a twist of a thorn,
Waiting for droplets, even a dew-drenched morn.

Banshee winds howl, but we're not scared at all,
Just sharing our secrets in the sun's golden pall.
"Do you know the one about the barrel cactus' plight?"
His party was canceled, no rain in sight!

We sip on the laughter over sips of the breeze,
Imagining shadows from winding, tall trees.
With every cracked piece of ground that we see,
We weave dreams of water like a shared cup of tea.

In this parched little pocket where humor's the key,
Life's dry spell becomes a bizarre jubilee.
On the edge of our seats, the punchline's unrolled,
The stories of drought turn to legends retold.

Prickly Companionship in Parched Lands

In a garden of pricks, friendship is found,
Among spiky companions, laughter does bound.
We poke gentle fun, oh what a delight,
Under the hot sun, we banter and fight.

With arms wide open, we embrace the heat,
Our humor like sunscreen, a tasty retreat.
Sharing our secrets in the still evening air,
Sarcastic whispers with a playful flare.

Through gusty winds and the sun's burning glare,
We lean in together, prepared for the dare.
With giggles and jabs, we create stories spun,
In this prickly jungle, mischief is fun!

So here's to our bond, oh isn't it sweet?
Each day is a riot, a delightful repeat.
In the midst of the dry, our hearts overflow,
With camaraderie and laughter, forever we grow.

Tales Told Through Thorned Lips

In the desert's grand parade,
The spines come out, unafraid.
With stories of pokes and prods,
They joke with sun and lazy gods.

Sipping rain in tiny sips,
Trading tales through thorny lips.
One prickle's poke turns into glee,
As laughter dances, wild and free.

With a wink, they wave the breeze,
Bound by ribs that aim to tease.
Eavesdropping on the moonlit night,
Whispers bloom 'neath stars so bright.

Among the rattles and the grins,
They spin their tales, where fun begins.
For every prick they hold, they learn,
That laughter is the best return.

Firm Roots in Shifting Sands

Rooted deep in the wobbly ground,
Where laughter echoes, oh so profound.
They dance in jest, with jagged pride,
Finding humor where gusts collide.

Each gust a joke, each breeze a pun,
In the desert heat, they know how to run.
Plant your feet, let's have some fun,
Whisper secrets till the day is done.

The watchers giggle as shadows sway,
Shifting sand makes the best buffet.
With roots so firm, yet always shifting,
They prank the winds, their voices lifting.

A tumble here, a breeze that bends,
The only rule? Make merry friends.
For laughter is the light in the heat,
In the shifting sands, they find their beat.

The Gentle Art of Defiance

With spines that say, 'Do not touch me',
They laugh at foes of every degree.
In their prickly coats, they find their might,
Turning stings into playful bites.

A dash of sass in every stem,
Defying drought with a cheeky gem.
They strut their stuff, with giggles loud,
Unbothered, they survive, fiercely proud.

When storms rush in with bluster and roar,
They shrug their spines and ask for more.
In battle stance, they throw a quip,
As petals dance and roots tight grip.

It's a quirky dance of boldness bright,
With every jab, they find delight.
Though nature tries to knock them down,
In the game of laughs, they wear the crown.

A Dialogue of Survival and Shadows

In twilight's grip, the shadows play,
With whispers low and humor gay.
Conversations bloom beneath the stars,
As chortles echo from cactus jars.

A gentle poke becomes a jest,
In survival's game, they jest the best.
Amidst the bounty of moonlit greens,
They swap their quirks, like silly machines.

With every rattle, they share a laugh,
Plotting pranks, crafting their own path.
In a world where water's scarce and few,
They toast to life with each dew they brew.

So here's to the companions of night,
With prickly wit and spirits bright.
In shadows deep, their joy unfolds,
Through tales of thorns, which they uphold.

Conversations Under Starlight

In the desert, whispers float,
Prickly pals swap tales, no note.
A cactus giggles, sways with grace,
Under the moon, a spiky embrace.

Laughter travels on the breeze,
Spines with secrets, oh, what tease!
One says, "Did you hear the deal?"
Another quips, "No way, unreal!"

Stars peek down, their glow so high,
Tales of love, lost in the sky.
With each jab and playful poke,
The night wraps them, a joke bespoke.

As the night falls, shadows play,
They share their dreams in bright display.
Jokes grow tall, like arms they wave,
In the quiet, they'll misbehave.

Thorns Tell Tales

Old thorny tales, they weave and spin,
Like a bard with tales to win.
A sprout insists, "I am the best!"
While the tall one grumbles, full of jest.

"You think you're sharp?" the short one cries,
"Well, look at me, I take the prize!"
With every prick, they start to tease,
Banter flows like a desert breeze.

"Remember the time we met that snake?"
"Yeah, it almost gave me a heart quake!"
The laughter echoes through the night,
As thorns shine bright, a funny sight.

In this prickly circle, joys expand,
With stories woven, hand in hand.
Each sharp remark brings endless glee,
In the realm of spines, they roam free.

Beyond the Green

Out in the wild, where shadows stretch,
A group of spines is set to sketch.
They gather closely, share a grin,
With tales of sun and playful sin.

One shouts, "I've grown three inches tall!"
While another replies, "That's not all!"
Funny moments, laughs abound,
In this world where joy is found.

The sun sets low, casting lines,
Their humor sharp, like pointed vines.
"Who knew being green could be this fun?"
The night is young; the jokes outrun.

"Do you think we got enough light?"
"Only if we're funny tonight!"
Amidst the prickle and the giggle,
They dance through dark, a hilarious wiggle.

Punctuated Silence

In the stillness, spines align,
Each waiting for a witty sign.
A pause, a look, then bursts of cheer,
As one begins, the end is near.

With every poke, they find their beat,
A punchline sharp, oh, isn't it sweet?
Absurdity grows in the desert air,
Spiky friends laughing without a care.

"Why did the plant cross the sand?"
"To get to the other prickly stand!"
Unexpected quips, they fly and swoop,
In this circle, they share a loop.

As starlit bursts fill the night,
They relish in this joyful rite.
Every silence, a chance to shine,
In the realm where thorns intertwine.

Dialogues in the Dunes

In the desert, two cacti chat,
One says, 'I lost my favorite hat!'
'Where'd it go?' the other inquires,
'Oh, it blew away in the wind's wild fires.'

They laugh under the sun's bright light,
'Next time, I'll add a cactus kite!'
'But won't it just stick to your spine?'
'That's a risk; my style's divine!'

As shadows stretched in sandy hue,
One asked, 'What do we do with blue?'
The other laughed, a pointy grin,
'Beats me! Let's start a cactus gym!'

'No weights, just hugs from prickly friends,'
'Maybe that's where the fun transcends!'
They danced and swayed, a thorny spree,
With giggles echoing wild and free.

Thorns of Thought

A cactus stood, deep in thought,
Wondering why warmth can't be bought.
Another joined, all dressed in spines,
'Stop pondering, let's sip some vines!'

'Vines? Are you sure they're nice to taste?'
'Of course, it's all about the haste!'
They made a drink of prickly glee,
And laughed at the mess for all to see.

One said, 'This drink tastes like despair!'
The other roared, 'Just don't breathe air!'
They clinked their arms, a jagged toast,
'For all the thorns that help us coast!'

So they sipped with joy and jest,
In the land where being prickly is best.
Laughing loud, with no regret,
Two quirky friends, the perfect set.

Silent Sentries

Two sentries stood, so tall and proud,
Guarding secrets from the crowd.
One whispered low, 'What's your plan?'
'Not much, just wait for a passing man.'

'What if they come with a watering can?'
'Then we play dead, like only we can!'
They chuckled softly, no one to hear,
With silence rich, they had no fear.

Amongst the sands, they watched the day,
While insects buzzed in a busy fray.
One sighed, 'I'd like a vacation, you know?'
'Not me; I'd miss the cactus show!'

'What show is that?' as the other grinned,
'Oh, you know, the one where we pretend to be pinned!'
With snickers shared, their laughter soared,
Invisible joy, by friendship ignored.

Prickly Ponderings

In the sun-drenched soil, they pondered their fate,
A cactus spoke, 'This life is first-rate!'
Another chirped, 'Unless it rains too much!'
Then we'll be mud pies, sticky and such!'

'Let's plan for sun and dance in the light,'
'How about a salsa under moon's height?'
They practiced steps, with a wobbly sway,
And laughed off the thorns that came out to play.

One said, 'I need a partner with flair!'
'Then find a bloom, we can style with care!'
They twirled and spun in a prickly mess,
With flowers dressing their pointy finesse.

'Why be dull when we can shine bright?'
'Let's paint our world with colors of light!'
With giggles and jabs, they found their groove,
Two prickly pals, always on the move.

Thorns in the Breeze

In a desert so dry, with sun in the sky,
A prickly bunch giggles, oh my, oh my!
With a jab and a poke, they joke in the heat,
'Do you think we can dance? Just don't crush our feet!'

Spines waving like palms, oh what a sight,
They sway to the rhythm, it's quite a delight.
A tumbleweed laughs, it rolls on by slow,
'You can't have a party, don't steal our show!'

A lizard joins in with a flip and a jump,
While a cactus spills water and makes quite a thump.
'Next time bring drinks, it's a dry, thirsty land,'
The pricks chuckle loudly, it's all cleverly planned.

By sunset they huddle, they share in their laughs,
Debating on hats made of funny, dry grass.
With thorns in the breeze, they keep stealing the scene,
A prickly parade, what a quirky routine!

In the Company of Spines

Gathered they are, in a quirky old bunch,
Having a chat while they sit down to lunch.
'I'm taller than you!' says the saguaro so proud,
While the barrel cactus grins, basking in loud.

'With all of your height, you just cast a big shade,
We've got spines like armor, we're the tough brigade!'
The hedgehog laughs softly, his quills all a-twitch,
'Let's settle this quickly, with a tall-standing pitch.'

With witty remarks, and no room for strife,
They poke gentle fun, making jokes about life.
'Do you think we're weird? With all this hard shell?'
The prickly pear giggles, 'At least we're not dull!'

In the company formed, each sharp line they share,
They crown each other kings, without a single care.
Plant pals in the sun, this gang is quite fine,
It's all in good humor, living life on a vine.

Whispers of the Arid Oasis

In the hush of the noon, when the sun's at its peak,
The spiky crew gathers, their playful technique.
'Do you hear that soft sound? It's the breeze in delight,'
Whispers of laughter, tickled by light.

The agaves are swaying, with wisdom they boast,
'We're sharp but so clever, we make the best toast!'
A crested bloom chimes in, with a nod and a wink,
'Just don't bring the water—we'll sink like a brick!'

Jokes fly like shadows, beneath the hot rays,
Each thorn-laden chuckle lights up the dry days.
'What do you call cacti who can never fit in?'
'Pointy and fabulous, thin skin on their grin!'

Oasis of mirth, where spines share a tale,
Bantering and bouncing, they dance without fail.
A prickly profession, these friends like to say,
Life's fun in the sun, in such quirky display!

Together in the Dry

Beneath the vast sky, in their arid retreat,
A crew of sharp dwellers meet for a treat.
'What's your secret?' one asks with a tilt of the head,
'To stay so so lively while roots stay in bed?'

Laughter erupts like a fountain of joy,
As they bounce and they poke, each gal and each boy.
'We've learned how to thrive on the sun's warm embrace,
With humor and jests, we're quick in the race!'

'Do you ever feel lonely, just stuck in the ground?'
'Only when I'm thirsty, and friends aren't around!'
They giggle and chortle, spines poking in glee,
'Together we bloom, and that's key to the spree!'

As dusk paints the sky, they share one last laugh,
In the dry desert song, they dance 'round with gaff.
In the arms of the sun, this family resides,
Together forever, with humor as guides!

Unwavering Whispers

In the desert, they stand so tall,
Chattering softly, they never fall.
Pointy hats on their spiky heads,
Sharing secrets where no one treads.

One told a joke, it was quite dry,
Another just laughed, oh my, oh my!
With each prick of their thorny skin,
A giggle escaped, let the fun begin!

They argue on who has the best shade,
While sunbathers fear the choices made.
Shimmery mirage tickles the eyes,
Their banter brightens desert skies.

In this prickly crew, joy is the game,
With the silliest stories and no one to blame.
So tip your hat to those spiny friends,
Their laughter will echo as daylight ends.

Tales from Thickets

In the thickets, they tell their tales,
Of windy days and sunlit gales.
One claimed to be the tallest of all,
While another just giggled, "You'll never fall!"

They swap wild stories of creatures so bizarre,
Dancing with lizards, dreaming of stars.
A tumbleweed rolls by with great flair,
And they all burst out laughing, unaware.

With each friendly poke, comes a hearty cheer,
"Let's stick together; we've nothing to fear!"
They preen and they prickle, a riot of fun,
As shadows grow long and bask in the sun.

So next time you wander where things grow wild,
Listen closely, as they behave like a child.
For in the thickets, laughter does sprout,
With tales that will leave you giggling about.

Barrenness and Beauty

In a place thought empty, life's on display,
With beauty wrapped in barbs, come what may.
A bloom bursts forth, so bold and bright,
Painting the world in sheer delight.

One plant exclaimed, "Look at this flower!"
The others all cheered, basking in power.
They giggled and danced like no one could see,
In a land where they thrive, wild and free.

Yet amidst the sharpness and prickly fun,
They boast about victories, one by one.
"A drought can't stop us; we're here to survive!"
With each new sunbeam, the plants come alive.

So if you feel stuck in a thorny situation,
Remember the laughter, the root of creation.
For beauty can flourish in barren lands,
A delightful reminder for weary hands.

Conversations Through Spines

In the cool of the shade, whispers arise,
From spikes and from tongues that seem to chastise.
"Did you hear what he said?" one prickly sage mocks,
While others all listen, like curious fox.

A wise old plant with a twisty grin,
Announced, "Here's a riddle, let the fun begin!"
With each quip and jest, their spines stand so proud,
Echoes of laughter ring out so loud.

They trade witty banter, sharp as their thorns,
While crickets do play their soft little horns.
"Who needs a hug when you've got a spine?"
A sprout piped up, "I'm feeling just fine!"

So let's toast to the thorns that keep us in line,
In a world full of laughs, where the sun always shines.
For conversations in gardens can be quite a treat,
When surrounded by friends who are prickly and sweet.

Consumed by the Drought

In the desert sands, they stand so tall,
Cracking jokes while soaking sun, not all.
Their thirsty roots, a bit of a twist,
'You call this a drought? I call it a mist!'

One cactus joked, 'I'm feeling quite dry,
I'm more of a sponge than a prickly guy!'
'Let's hold a party, right here by the dune,'
'Bring the water, and we'll dance in the noon!'

The lizards laughed as they joined the fun,
Cactuses twisted, swayed, and spun.
Who needs hydration when laughter's the key?
In the sun's embrace, we're perfectly free!

So here's to the drought, with humor in play,
Our spiky selves finding joy every day!
In this parched land, we flourish and thrive,
With punchlines and puns, we come alive!

Beside Fiery Blooms

Beside bold petals, our laughter swells,
We prickle and poke, and share our tales.
'You see that bloom? It's trying too hard!'
'Some charm just lives in the prickly yard!'

With colors that pop, we're the jesters here,
Daring the blossoms to bring it, we cheer!
'With thorns like these, we can't play by the rules,'
'These flowers are cute, but we're the cool fools!'

The sun blares down, but we don't mind,
Sipping the heat, we're far too blind.
'Hey, pink daisy, you're a shade of bright,
But who can outshine our prickle delight?'

So let's raise a glass by the fiery blooms,
To laughs, to joy, and the spiky plumes!
In laughter and shade, we find our way,
It's all about fun in this green cabaret!

Silent Vigil under Sun

Under the sun, we hold a pact,
No words exchanged; it's a silent act.
Yet in our stillness, the humor grows,
As we pose for pictures, striking a pose!

One cactus thought, 'Is that a cactus wren?
I swear, if it lands, I'll just pretend!'
With each blink of sun, we make our stand,
Contemplating life—armored and grand.

Stillness abounds, yet giggles seep,
As shadows play tricks, like whispers in sleep.
A lizard meanders, then stops with a turn,
'Even in silence, there's wisdom to learn!'

So we vigil together, beneath the bright rays,
Finding joy in the moments, and quirky delays.
In giggles and grins, we quietly dwell,
For under the sun, we're living so well!

The Heart Beneath

Deep in the thorns, we hide a soft core,
Those prickly exteriors open no door.
Yet humor shows lightly in every sway,
'Behind this tough shell, there's more than one way!'

'You think I'm tough? Well, take a close look,
There's a heart that beats in this thorny nook!'
As petals wither and bits start to fly,
We giggle and poke, 'A bruised heart won't die!'

Amidst every prickle, a twinkle does peek,
In laughter and joy, we find what we seek.
'Why worry so much when you're this darn cute?
With humor and heart, we make our own loot!'

So here's to the heart beneath prickly walls,
With laughter that echoes, we stand proud, we stand tall!
In every tough moment, we shine and we jest,
For life's full of love when we're simply at best!

The Desert's Chorus

Underneath the baking sun,
The prickly ones stand and hum.
Their spines do tap a funny tune,
While lizards dance and cacti fume.

With every wind that blows them flat,
They wiggle close and share a chat.
One says, 'Did you hear the joke?'
The other laughs till it nearly broke.

A flower blooms to join the fray,
'I'm not a weed, please let me stay!'
They giggle and sway with such delight,
As shadows stretch into the night.

So in this land so dry and wide,
The thorny friends enjoy the ride.
With every quip they exchange and jest,
In the desert sun, they feel the best.

Unraveled Stories

In the land where the cactus grows,
A tale of laughter softly flows.
One sassy spine speaks up with cheer,
'I've got a secret, come lend an ear!'

'Last summer, a bird lost her way,
She perched on me for a whole day!'
Though she claimed it was just for rest,
The prickles sure were not impressed.

Another chimed with a shrug and grin,
'Why do we always let flies in?
They buzz and tease, then swoop around,
Why not kick them out, we're thorn-bound!'

With stories tangled like their limbs,
They share the laughs, their life not dim.
In every heart, a chuckle blooms,
In this dry land, joy brightly looms.

Tales of the Thorny Ones

Gathered round in the afternoon,
The spiky ones croon a playful tune.
'What's sharp and sweet, and kills the gloom?'
A bold one boasts, 'Let's find that bloom!'

They poke and tease each other bright,
With silly antics that bring delight.
'Who needs a garden?' a wise one calls,
'Here in the dirt, we break down walls!'

With jovial ribs and bits of sass,
They laugh at things that come to pass.
Under the sun, no room for pout,
In their green world, they dance about.

So let's raise a glass of mirth today,
To those that thrive where the dry winds play.
In every point and quirky spin,
The stories told are bound to win.

Harmony in the Dryland

In a garden where the sun won't hide,
The poky bunch sits side by side.
With stories shared in prickly wit,
They entertain, no need to quit.

'Why did the cactus cross the sand?
To find the punchline, isn't it grand?'
They laugh aloud, with no disdain,
For in this jest, there's joy to gain.

They poke at time, they laugh with glee,
'We're not just plants, we're family!'
Each spine a part of this grand show,
In the vast dryland, their spirits glow.

So if you wander where they stand tall,
Remember their laughter, embrace it all.
For in this land of sun and fun,
The harmony shines when day is done.

Interwoven Spines of Understanding

In the desert where we stand,
Two prickly friends lend a hand.
With laughter echoing through the sand,
Each joke a thistle, cleverly planned.

Riddles shared in silence bloom,
As we dance beneath the moon.
Our sharp remarks like puns in plume,
Twisting tales, creating a room.

With every poke, we find delight,
In the quirky scenes of night.
Who knew that spines could spark a fight?
Yet here we are, all feeling bright.

So let's toast in this sun-blushed place,
To the funny fits of our embrace.
In our sharpness, there's warmth and grace,
Two prickles weaving into space.

Cracked Earth

The ground beneath us holds a pact,
In every fracture, there's a fact.
We share our woes, no need to act,
Our laughter's loud, the best distract.

With every drought, we joke and tease,
In woven tales, we find our ease.
Though some may wilt, and others freeze,
Our humor blossoms like the breeze.

We giggle at the sun's cruel games,
And dance around with silly names.
Who knew the dirt could hold such claims,
Of wit and whimsy, joy in flames?

So let the earth be cracked and bare,
With stories told, we have our share.
In barren lands, we freely dare,
To find the joy hiding out there.

Deep Words

We sink our roots in sandy sheets,
With whispered thoughts, our humor greets.
In depths below, the laughter meets,
And grows like plants on tiny seats.

Each quip a thorn, each grin a bloom,
As sharp and funny thoughts consume.
We twist our tales, dispel the gloom,
In this dry old patch, we find our room.

With wisdom sprouting from our sides,
In every jab, a truth resides.
Our banter spreads on nature's tides,
And still, we thrive where humor guides.

So listen close among the green,
For deep words sprout from all unseen.
In playful jests, we're rarely mean,
Together, we're a funny team.

Hushed Meetings Beneath the Stars

In quiet hours, the shadows dance,
Two friends share a sarcastic glance.
With winks and puns, we take a chance,
To laugh aloud in this vast expanse.

The stars above, a watching crowd,
As words flit by, both sharp and loud.
In twinkling skies, we're humor's proud,
In prickly tones, we're not too cowed.

Amidst the vastness, we plant our dreams,
With silly thoughts, we burst the seams.
For in this friendship, laughter streams,
A night of joy, or so it seems.

So let the cosmos hear our cheer,
In every jab, we hold so dear.
With twirls and laughs, we persevere,
Under the stars, we're spikes of cheer.

The Dialogues of Drying Blooms

In sunshine bright, we flake and fade,
Our petals crisp in a colorful parade.
Yet even wilting can be played,
With chuckles shared, the memories laid.

Our chat's a breeze, a gentle tease,
As colors dull, we still feel ease.
For every thorn, a joke appease,
In fading blooms, we find such trees.

So let the petals fall away,
For laughter's light will always stay.
In drying jokes, we find our play,
As humor shines a bright array.

Together, even as we wilt,
We share our tales, no need for guilt.
In every laugh, a bond is built,
With funny fronds, our joy is spilt.

Secrets in the Sprawling Silence

In a desert sun, they stand so tall,
Whispering secrets, to one and all.
Their silent chatter, oh, what a scene,
Sharing jokes between the green.

A guy named Spike cracks a wise old pun,
He tickles the air; the laughter's begun.
"With no arms to hug, I still feel the love,
Just don't get too close, or it's push, shove!"

The sand laughs back with a rascally glee,
"Who knew your jokes would be just for me?"
"Next time bring water, not just the mirth,
I need hydration, it's dry on this Earth!"

So they chuckle and jest, in the bright desert light,
With prickly hearts and spirits so bright.
In the sprawling silence, they share their delight,
These silent stand-ups, a true comic sight.

Spinal Stories

Under the sun, they've got back pains,
Stories bend like their spiny veins.
"Oh, my branches ache! What a night!"
"Tell me, friend, how'd you survive the fright?"

"With a pair of shoes and a bottle of spray,
A dance hall now, but a cactus ballet!"
"Was it a good time? Did you get in the groove?"
"Not with these thorns; I can't even move!"

They share their tales of nighttime glories,
Flexing their spines with back-breaking stories.
"Ouch! Watch your step, I just planted a joke,
If you slip and fall, you'll become a poke!"

But laughter erupts under the clear blue,
"Your humor is prickly, it's really quite true!"
With every story, they stand tall and proud,
A spine-tingling scene, cacti in a crowd.

Echoes of a Prickly Past

In the wind, they hear echoes of laughs,
Stories from tales of their spiny crafts.
"Remember last week, the tumbleweeds rolled?
They begged us for cover; they're really quite bold!"

"Those winds are cheeky, they blow all around,
Once blew my hat clear across the ground!
Then I stood still, with a grin on my face,
While the others just whirled in a dizzying race!"

Underneath stars, they trust and confide,
Sharing their quips with prickly pride.
"One day I'll dance with the moonlight's glint,
No thorns or worries; I'll just be a hint!"

So they chuckle with glee, under cool night's cast,
Tales of humor—an echo from the past.
Together they stand, no fear of the night,
With laughter like spikes, they shine, oh so bright.

Conversations with Shadows

In twilight's glow, shadows begin to play,
Whispering secrets, come out and stray.
"Are you tripling up, or are we just one?
Don't hide in the darkness; let's have some fun!"

"Oh no, dear shadow, I'm just a tall soul,
With stories to tell, let's roll as a whole!"
"Let's take the plunge, dance 'til we tire,
Twisting and twirling, our dreams set on fire!"

As shadows entwine, they laugh and they glide,
Making mischief alongside the moon's ride.
"Can you imagine a world where we're free,
A cactus can dance, whirling serious glee?"

With a sprinkle of starlight, laughter ensues,
Their prickly tales take hilarious cues.
For in the shadows, they're never alone,
In this funny fiesta, their hearts have grown.